Ready or Not

Living in the Break Down Lane

By

Paul Richmond

Published by Human Error Publishing
Paul Richmond
www.humanerrorpublishing.com
paul@humanerrorpublishing.com

P O Box 838
Greenfield, MA 01302

Copyright © 2009 by Paul Richmond
All Rights Reserved

ISBN: 978-0-9833344-0-8

First Edition June 2009

Printed in the United States of America

Human Error Publishing asks that no part of this
publication be reproduced or transmitted in any form
or by any means, electronic or mechanical, including
photocopy, recording or information storage or retrieval
system without permission in writing from the publisher.
the reason, the author needs the money.

Front and Back Cover Collages by Pablo
Front cover lay out and title was a collaboration with
Waffles T Clown

Paul Richmond has published a glossy-covered little book of irreverent, funny poems. He calls them "stories," and they are that too, most with a moral, or a peek into we all would be seconds if we were merchandise. He writes in a really loose, train-of-consciousness style that is easy to follow, inexplicably hilarious, and reminds me of Ginsberg and Beat poetry. The book is R-rated. Jonathan von Ranson

Quirky stories & revealing surprises abound here. Short and packed with meaning, these are stories to be savored. One can almost see them as performance pieces. Protest art. Surreal emotional moments. Paradoxical portraits. This author has a strong and unique voice. Great collage art on the covers. A rare book, worth seeking out. As the author states, "The secrets that are revealed in this book will change everyone's life around you. Unfortunately you have to change your own life." VisionWorks - Dick Mcleester

The first time I saw Paul Richmond, I was a judge for a poetry competition for the Florence Poets Society. There were a lot of great poems that day, also many pretty awful ones. As soon as I saw Paul, I knew something was up with this guy. He had a "look' to him like I was really in for something. One of those funny glowing aura things you see around an intensely creative person. Well I was right. His words were awesome, his delivery a beautiful thing, and he made me think about things while making me laugh heartily at the same time. I immediately bought his book and had him sign it and have been a huge fan ever since. Pick up a copy of everything this guy has ever written, I promise you will not be disappointed!! To see him perform live is an absolutely wonderful experience also.
Peter Smolenski - Abstract Artist – Creator of Global Online Art and Poetry events

Hello

Ready or Not
Living in The Break Down Lane

Was written

1) In the back of a stolen car
- That was parked in a field -
That I lived in for a summer

2) While breaking up - Losing
my job - Losing my home -
Realizing I had no friends - In a
workshop meant to build self-esteem.

3) By an unknown author for they were all in a weather
beaten notebook - Found on a table in a café - They
have just been copied here

4) While listening to jazzzzzzzz - Stoned - In bits and
pieces - In a delusional time - When I considered myself
a writer

Actually there is no need for you to know how and
where these were written. That is for another time,
when fans ask for the biography. For now I hope you
enjoy them. That they inspire you. After reading these
you might wonder, ask, why am I not writing? As with
all things, these pages contain material which might
inspire you to express your point of view. Each of you
may argue that your vision is the one to follow and
since each of you has a unique prophecy, this will lead
to heated discussions.

In order to help with these discussions, I suggest that you and everyone you know have a copy of this book. That way it can be studied in search of clues. What you will find I can assure you is not what you were looking for and I am afraid to say I don't know where to tell you to look. It is said, "it", can be found within each of us.

If you go on this treasure hunt, I am not responsible for any spiritual awakening that might or might not take place.

In dedication to my men's group, I open this book with,10 Men

I am glad to be alive

Paul Richmond

Contents

10 Men

9 men
One is missing
That would make 10

What do these men do together?
They meet
Once a month
They sit
They talk
They swim
They drink
They smoke
They get high together
They cry
They laugh
They listen
They sleep
They represent years
And years together

They have seen each other

What do they talk about?
Their need for love
Aliens
How to solve the world's problems
How to solve their own problems
They find answers together
They acknowledge the unanswered
They recharge
Experience their brotherhood
The missing one
Is missed
For they are 10 Men

2012- Max Out The Credit Cards

2012 is the year
It is said to be the end
Of life as we know it

It is said there will be pole shifts
That the Earth's Plates will move
25 years of darkness is predicted

Some would say
The shit is going to hit the fan

Not sure how many of us will be around
2012 is only 4 years away
Each day being a gift
So what does this mean?
If the whole scene is going to crash
This might be the time
To take all my credit cards
To their max
Come to think of it
They are at their max

If it doesn't crash
I'll have a lot to pay back
So then I find myself hoping it will crash
Since I will be up shit's creek if it doesn't crash
Yet I don't really want it to crash
I want my imprint to help sustain
Not tear down

Create safety
Not more fear

Create peace
Not endless wars

Celebrate freedoms
Not more repression

Tic Tic Tic
Yes the clock is ticking
Tic Tic Tic
Bombs go off

2012
Where will you be?
What will you do until then?
Will you speak out against the injustices?

2012 is said to be the end
Of life as we know it
If you are reading / hearing this
And it is
2013
I am glad it didn't crash
Or maybe it did
And
You are one of the survivors
All I can say is
Don't max out the credit cards

A Dusty Old Town

Off highway 93
Pray for me I am on highway 93
Is heard as a local greeting
We are here for the town parade
We are standing in the 90 degree shade
At the last turn where the parade ends

The parade is made up of
Police cars, letting their sirens wail
Many of the native people
And the poor white
Hear this wailing in their daily lives
Why anyone thinks they would want to hear it
At the parade
Is anyone's guess
Could be to celebrate
That for now the police aren't coming after them

Fire trucks spray us with water
Everyone screams with happiness
For it is another day over a hundred degrees

There are some floats
On flat bed trucks
They throw candy
There is a car with Miss Montana waving
There are floats with themes
One is
Two men sitting out at a campfire
Cooking
Off to the side of them is a tree
In the tree are a number of ropes

Used for hanging
In one of the ropes there is a man hanging

A woman standing next to me boos
Yells at the people driving the float
Asking why show this scene?
She yells
Isn't the parade for the children?
She keeps booing
I look at the float
It is unclear to me
What the float is about
Is it what the Wild West was like?
Or still is?

As I stood on the street corner
A man stumbles up to me
Makes eye contact
His speech is mumbled
His hands waved around
He was obviously saying something
He wanted to interact
I was standoffish
As if not knowing what this drunk guy would do
I somehow wanted to help him
He said he was born in this dusty town
Said his mother died of cancer
He sat down on the sidewalk
Continued to wave his hands
Looking straight at me
As if seeing through me
That I was moving on
I could walk away
I could leave this dusty town

A Sunny Saturday

What goes on?

It means a day off
For some

People out in the streets
Men walking with their chests out
Varoommm Varoommm
The loud sounds of the motorcycles
The constant gassing of the engines
As if to roar
Make one's presence known
Guys hanging out together, drinking
Yelling loudly
Swearing, Swearing, Swearing
One guy keeps punching everyone
Keeps trying to get the others to react
Cars, motorcycles speeding by
Violence in their speed
The noise
How they stand
Defining their territory

They weren't there to enjoy the sun

Aren't You Interested?

He said Hi
She said try someone else
He said my name is Love
She said I have heard it before
He said this time it is real
She said I have heard that before too
He said I know you're the one
She said for what
He said for walking into sunsets
She said it feels like it's going to rain
He said I have an umbrella
She said it's not big enough for both of us
He said I'll use it to cover you
She said I don't want to feel guilty
He said it was nice talking to you
She said what's the matter
Aren't you interested?

Bagging Groceries

I was in the supermarket
Checking out
I noticed the person bagging my food
We got to talking
He was in his nineties
I asked why was he here bagging groceries
He said
I have bills
And I am not dead yet

Contest

What are the rules?

Knowing the rules
One feels one has a fair chance
To do their best
To win

In Wars
Rules have been created
In the attempt
To define what is fair
How the killing can be done
As if to contain the savagery
Of "anything goes"

War is
The closest step to
Anything goes

There is the fear
That horror will reign

And
It does

And
There are no winners

Crossing The Line

He looks up and notices
That the driver coming towards him
Is crossing the double yellow line
Right into his lane
Is this person drunk?
Or is this person doing what he normally does
Looking through his bag
Reaching for his cell phone
Can't find matches

As the driver coming towards him
Swerves their car to their side of the road
They pass each other without hitting
He tells himself he worries about other drivers
As he reaches down to find his water bottle
As his car swerves
Skims a pole
Takes out a few sign posts
Back on the road as if nothing had happened

He wonders how can you get people to change?

Do You Swear?

Do you swear?
To tell the truth
The whole truth
Nothing but the truth
So help you God

Our first leader
George Washington
Chopped down a cherry tree
And when he was asked
He couldn't tell a lie
He said he did it
I am supposed to use that as an example
Of a great leader's character
To never tell a lie
Yet he chopped down the cherry tree
A source of food
For no reason

No reason was ever given
Just that he couldn't lie
So he admitted doing it
Why?
He didn't like cherries?
What's not to like about cherries?
I think it was the first sign of aggression
He let it out by attacking the environment
He just didn't lie about it

Now when our modern leaders
Do their version
Of chopping down the cherry tree
They just lie
People know they chopped down the cherry tree

Our modern leaders respond
There was never a tree there

It's established there was a tree
They knew nothing about it

They release possible scenarios
The tree must have fallen over by itself
Maybe due to a powerful wind

When evidence of wood chips are found
Where the tree used to be
They respond
We have to do something about those pesky beavers

They are informed that all the beavers have died
Suddenly a boy scout is arrested
Said to have been on drugs
Searching his room
It is reported he listened to music about Satan

Notes were found, scribbled
On hundreds of girl-scout cookie boxes
From the girl-scout who sold him the cookies

The notes were
Rejections of his pleas
For her to be his cookie

It is reported we have caught
The Terrorist
After hearing this on the news
I am supposed to feel relieved
The problem has been solved
The guilty have been caught
And will be punished

The next day

Another tree is missing

Do you swear?
To tell the truth
The whole truth
Nothing but the truth
So help you God

Feeling The Pressure

He said I can't remember my password

She says
Without your password
The bombs will go off in 10 seconds
The world will be destroyed
All will be lost

What she really said was
I am getting my period
So you better Fucking remember your password

Gas Station

An old beat up station wagon
Pulls in
To a gas station
A woman driver
A male passenger
A little white dog
In a cage
In the back seat
With a very high pitched bark
Shut up
The woman screams
The guy is hitting the cage
Shut up
The woman screams
The guy is hitting the cage
The little white dog
In the cage
Is barking
The woman and the man
Looked like they hadn't
Seen a smile in years

I just stopped to get gas

Too Good To Be True

He was in his fifties
She was in her thirties
She was beautiful
She persuaded him
They were meant for each other
She told him she used birth control
She gave him a blow job
They had intercourse
She arrived a few months later
She was pregnant
She hadn't used any birth control
She needed a green card
He married her
She turned out to be crazy
Both of her parents committed suicide
Now all she wants to do is cut off his balls
Something told him it was too good to be true

Just Beginning

He heard someone call out
Old man do you need some help?

He went to look around
Who was the old man who needed help?

He then noticed that he was looking up at
people
Who were looking down at him
He was lying on the ground
Not remembering how he got there
Could this really be the end?
He had felt he was just beginning

A Bad Connection

Everything you want me to say

I can't say

Everything I want to say

You're not listening

Feeling Alive

I was leaving a warm house
I wanted to experience
Feeling Alive
I wanted to go to this event
It was an hour away
I assumed it would be like any other day
I would just get in my car and drive there

It had snowed and it was a wet snow
The trees were sagging from the weight
As I drove snow fell
Like ice balls
Like the ones bullies
Used to throw at the bus stop
As I drove
I watch them hit the street in front of me
Could hear them hitting the roofs of the houses
As I drove by
It startled me when one hit the roof of the car
Was a real shocker when one hit the windshield
The windshield didn't shatter
I went a little further and the trees thinned out
The ice balls stopped
The road narrowed
Snow was piled on both sides
Around a turn a car came going a little too fast
Crossing over the double lines
With me hugging the line
Since there was no room due to the piled snow
They swerved back on to their side
We passed each other without hitting

Why did I ever leave my warm home?
I didn't want to miss the event
I wanted to feel alive
As I drove the chances for me to die
Seemed to keep increasing
The car started to slide
I was going right for that telephone pole
Suddenly I was not skidding
The pole was behind me
The ride continued in this eventful way
When I finally got there
I thanked my lucky stars

I then learned the event was canceled

The ride home was just as exciting
Took twice as long
On finally walking into my warm house
I thought to myself
It feels so good to be alive

Lost Wallet

When the camera zooms in
Our main character
Is just about to go out
Suddenly he realizes he doesn't have his wallet
The search begins
He traces his steps
Looks through his pockets
Opens up the bags he has with him
Looks in the car
Under the seat
It must have fallen out of his pocket
In retracing his steps
He thinks that he came home with it
That it has to be somewhere in the house
Now he's running out of time
He was going to go out
Meet some people

The camera zooms back
To take in more of the scene
And lying on a couch
Is a woman
They have been lovers
For 13 years
They have lived together
She was feeling low energy all day
On trying to figure out what they might do
He suggests meeting some friends
At a political talk
A Woman who has become
Famous for asking the President
Why did her son die in Afghanistan?

Why were we in the war?
She was here in town
Speaking at the local middle school

He asks did she want to go
She asks why?
To hear about how fucked up things were
She feels she knows what is going to be said
Isn't inspired by these talks
She doesn't want to go
Says she has no energy for anything
Nothing inspires her
She apologizes
Says it was nothing personal
She just doesn't have any energy
He doesn't try to make an argument for going
He is ready to go alone

Back to the lost wallet
Getting frustrated
He can't find it
He doesn't want his life to be like this
Looking for lost wallets
Life is going by, time is getting late
He has now searched the same places twice
Three times
He has to admit it wasn't anywhere to be found
He can't leave until he finds it

Suddenly feeling sick to his stomach
He goes to the bathroom
Diarrhea
Had the flu about a week ago
All of a sudden

He's in the bathroom again
On coming out
He thinks to look on the table again
He thought he took everything out of his pockets
He checks the table again
Starts to clear the table
He moves her purse and there it is
Her purse was on it
Now he has the wallet
But suddenly he needs to hit the john again
Thinking of his father
Who complains that he has diarrhea all the time
And blames it on a new food
That he thinks gave it to him
He thinks he's turning into his father
Then he looks at the clock
And realizes how much time has gone by
The event is starting
He is still standing in his kitchen
He is 30 minutes away
With more stomach rumblings
Feels like any moment
He will need to run to the john again
Not a great incentive to go out

This isn't quite the story line of a thriller
A cliffhanger
Where you are sitting on the edge of your seat
Instead our hero is sitting on the toilet
Wanting his life to mean something

No Love Letter Today

I went to the Post Office
To check my mail
Hoping I received a love letter
Parked in front of the Post Office
A big guy sitting in his car waiting next to mine
His car looks pretty beat up
He looks like he's been waiting for a while
A woman finally comes out of the post office
As she opens up the door to his car
She says something
He says something
Her voice gets loud
"I am not sitting on all of this crap"
He starts throwing things into the back seat
Her voice getting louder and louder
About all the crap
She's tired of the crap
That she's not going to sit in it
He's starting to yell
Things are flying
I wonder just how much crap
Can be on that front seat
Things are still flying
Finally she is waving him off
Getting into the car
Still complaining
Now he is really mad
She's making a scene
She's yelling
He pulls his car out really quickly
Tires screech
He floors it

Burning rubber down the street
As the car drives off
You can hear both of them yelling

I went into the post office
My mailbox was empty
No love letter today

Red White And Blue

We see Red
We call out
Do you see Red?
The camera zooms in
The experts are called in
The commissions are called
The investigations take place
Politicians act like politicians
Everyone already knows the outcome

We are told it is Blue
We know it is Red
We have seen the blood
We are told it is Blue

We look for the White light
In the Red White and Blue

Ruth Stone The Poet Laureate of VT

She was ninety-two
She was going blind
She had a hearing aid that didn't work well
Her daughter sat next to her
Wore glasses
Her daughter would read the first
And maybe the second line
She would then say the poems from memory
Asking for a line here and there
Her daughter sat with a folder of poems
They did a mother daughter dance
The mother saying one thing
The daughter saying another
The daughter would suggest a poem
The mother would say not that one
The daughter would say you like that one
This went on throughout the reading
The mother's answers were
I don't remember that one
That's too long
I don't like that one anymore
That's too sad
I want a funny one
I know I wrote funny ones
She said this many times
The daughter said
You're obsessed with wanting funny ones
She's 92
Can just barely see
Can't hear
Is dependent on everyone
On her daughter

She felt the crowd
Who took in her every word
She beamed at the applause
Blushed with the recognition
Said we were a forgiving audience
She said she wanted a funny one

You Want Me To Do What?

In a studio across town
A photographer
And
A young woman
Face each other
She said you want to pay me how much?
She said you want me to stand against the wall
Doing what?
You want me to bend over
You want me to shake my ass
You want me to stretch out my leg
You want me to be caressing my thigh
Take off my clothes
Wear this skimpy outfit
To stand around in my underwear
To pose
And pucker my lips
She negotiated for more money

Thousands of miles away in a war zone
A squadron of military personal
10 guys and one woman stood guard
They were on this hill
Guarding nothing
They were there for hours
It was extremely boring
The guys decided to collect money among them
There wasn't much
They knew she liked M&M's
They got her some
And they asked her
To take off her top
She felt hurt

She really cared for all of these guys
They were a team
She would have done anything for them
She would have considered
Taking off her top for nothing
The fact that they wanted to pay her
She felt hurt
It really hurt

In a living room
A couple sitting together on a couch
She says
Honey
You want me to do what?
She said
It's been a long day
Why don't we curl up on the couch
Watch a movie
Maybe I'll shake my ass tomorrow

The Real Criminals

Your Honor
I would like to say
That in this case
There is more than just
The overwhelming evidence
Of my guilt
There are other factors
That I would like to highlight

But first I would like to ask
That your Honor would adjourn the court
Until a much later date
So I may have the time
To come up with what they are

Since your Honor is unwilling to adjourn
Let me say
The fact that my accusers have compiled
Thousands upon thousands of pages
Of documentation
Besides the fact that I am seen on video
That there are many pictures of me
Being caught in the act

All pales to the clear explanation
I am about to give

Once this explanation is given and understood
It will shed a new light
On my character
Which by the way is of being helpful

You may be asking yourselves
What could this explanation possibly be

Your honor
I would like to put forth
As wild as it might seem
That there was actually another man
That I was not the lone gunman
That another man
Committed the crimes I am accused of

On walking into the crime scene
I happened upon this lowlife
That I thought was a gentleman
We exchanged a few social pleasantries
He confided in me that he was in a tough spot
That he had worked hard
To get himself where he was
He told me he was just about to reap
The fruits of his labor
But he had one problem
He needed to go to the bathroom
Obviously if he left to go to the bathroom
He wouldn't be there to reap his rewards
As he explains this
I could see him fidgeting
Which then led to jumping up and down
He obviously had to go badly
Knowing myself of the dilemma
I told him I would hold his place
In order to help out
While he ran off to relieve himself
He thanked me profusely
He assured me

I would receive what was coming to me
Your Honor
Regardless of all the evidence
We must open our eyes
To the conspiracies around us
To the secret governments
To the crimes and injustices being done
That my case pales against

The real criminals

How Things Worked Out

He said I am not going to be here my whole life
He said I'll stay a year or two
He and his wife were having their first kid
He told himself he was an artist
His creativity didn't pay the bills
Work was hard to find
There were openings at the factory
They had three girls
20 years flew by
He thought he would retire
From this factory job

The factory closed
He was jobless
His creativity had left him
He drank
His wife left him
Things didn't work out as he thought

The Note

He said If only the girl
Sitting in the desk next to me
Would notice me

The only interaction
I have with her
Is when she passes me a note
That I would fantasize was for me
She wants me to pass it on
To the boy on the other side of me

The boy who sits next to me
The one who the note is for
Could clean the playground with me
I don't dare to not give him the note
Or even think of reading it
That would be suicidal

She would look at me
When she was giving me the note
It was the only time she looked at me

As she looked at me
To give me the note
I would take a long look

He then said again
I would take a long look

He said I was tormented
As I held her steamy note
The loser in the middle

I heard this story
In a dimly lit bus station
From a sheepish guy
Who had one small suitcase
And a large bottle of cheap wine

To cheer him up
I told him the boy next to him
Died from some sexual disease
That the girl was a pole dancer
In a strip club
And she was single

I said to him there was still hope
He didn't believe me

And I don't think you should either

Want Ads

In the want ads
Speed rosary reciters are wanted
Times are bad
The only hope
Is to increase the number of rosaries
Prayers being said
In the hopes to keep up with the sinners

Speed rosary reciting
Has turned into a paying gig
Heavy competition for the job
One needs to go into training
To learn techniques to be able to speed rosary
On touring the church we are shown
Three speed rosary reciters battling it out
For who is the fastest
All you can hear is a whispering sound
smsmsmsmsmsmmsms

The sound I remember old ladies making
As their fingers move across the beads

Suddenly an argument breaks out
One is accusing the other of skipping a bead
While the two of them argue
They then notice the third is getting ahead
The one who does the most rosaries
Gets a bonus
So the two stop arguing
Try and distract the third
They succeed
Giving them a chance to catch up

The whispering gets louder and more frantic
It is rumored that the sinners are increasing
In the radical high tech section of this church
They are taping speed rosary reciters
So that they can be played back
Increasing the number of rosaries being said
Computers are used to enhance the recordings
In the hopes to speed them up
Some argue that this isn't prayer
Others argue
Prayer has been dead for centuries
The whispering is now deafening

I am asked do I want the job?

Being out of work and hungry
I decline
I decide to apply for the speed communion taking
This way I'd get paid
And I get to eat

As far as the sinners go
They have to live with themselves

When Your Heart Is On Fire

When your heart is on Fire
Smoke gets in your eyes
When your eyes drink of desire
Your mind pours gas on the fire
When the touch is soft and inviting
Temperatures rise
When you feel the heat
It's cooling to remove your clothes
When the heart beats, the blood pumps
When the hands wander, the mind surrenders
When the toes curl, the mouth goes dry
Try as we might
It's hard to let go
No No
We didn't say No
When your heart is on Fire
Smoke gets in your eyes

It's A Good Day When It's Garbage Day

I was standing on the corner
A homeless guy
Looks at me and says
It's a good day
When it's garbage day

Many all over the world find something to eat
Find clothes, items that they needed
Things they can sell
There is so much waste
There are so many with nothing
It's a good day
When it's garbage day

Sharing

I learned the value of sharing in Kindergarten
Where Miss Peters
Said to me
I needed to share my favorite blocks
With Billy

Billy was the boy
Who tormented me

Every block I found that was smooth
Curved
With the grains of the wood
Creating beauty and interesting patterns
Billy would take it from me
Billy didn't care about any of these things
He only cared about tormenting me
By taking each block I found

Billy liked to throw the blocks at me
Billy liked to chew on the blocks
Billy liked to draw on the blocks

Miss Peters said it would be good
For my character
That I needed to know how to share
I had to share my blocks with Billy

Miss Peters said
Sharing would make me feel good
What made me feel good
Was biting Billy
Miss Peters said I had to stop biting Billy
I said I was sharing
My feelings with Billy

He Waits

He's 90 years old
He's in a senior home
He says everyone else is in their 80's
He said they are at the end of their lives
Various stages of decay
He always thought he would die first
Before his wife
He didn't
He says that it's 3 to one
Women to men
The men do usually die first
He says they are all old ladies
Doesn't get his blood flowing
He talked of a younger woman
How special she was
He's just waiting now
He didn't want to leave his house
His kids made him move
When his wife, their mother died
At the time he says
He wasn't in any shape to fight back
He knows that there wasn't really
Any other alternative
He writes now
Little poems
And he waits

Didn't See A Way Out

I answered the phone
He said to me
I get treated like shit
And then
I am supposed to act all kissy poo
He said I don't feel kissy poo

I feel I was made to feel like a piece of shit
Does he have the right to react?
Not feel all kissy poo

What is an acceptable time?
To not feel kissy poo
She wants him to recover immediately
What is the big deal?
Why was he holding on to it?

He didn't like it
It wasn't the first time
It wouldn't be the last time
He wished it would change
He felt depressed that he knew it wouldn't
Luckily the house was big enough
He had somewhere to go

Others who lived in small apartments
Drank more
And fought more
There was violence
He sat by himself
He had his own projects
His art that kept his soul alive
Generally he felt beat down at every turn
He didn't see a way out

It Started So Moist

I stood in line in a drug store
Waiting to pay the cashier
There before everyone in the store
We watched as they stumbled into each other
Their eyes were down
Their lips were shut
Their tongues were not peeking out
To look at each other
Their heads immediately taking their bodies
In a different direction then toward each other

It had started so moist
Tongues playing
Lips wet
Giving way to all notions of reason
Was this allowed?
The question was asked by each of them
At the time
As their hands slide along
On each of their receptive bodies
There was judgment in the air

Where does your judgment fall?
Does it matter whose lips are touching?

A father and daughter
Or a mother and son
An uncle and niece
An aunt and cousin
An eighth grade teacher and student
A cheerleader and coach
A priest and altar boy

A nun and the custodian of the convent

The boy scout leader and his favorite boy scout
Grandpa and the girl scout
Who entered his house
To sell him some cookies
Grandma and the young cashier
Who worked in the supermarket
The nurse and the wounded solider
In the hospital
The soldier and his prisoner
The married man
Who was a boss with his secretary
A mother seducing her son's teenage friends
The father and the baby-sitter
The doctor and the nurse
The southern belle and teenage slave
The elected official and the town whore
Farmer Bob and good old Betsy in the barn

The 55-year-old man on the Internet
Saying he was 22
And the 17-year-old horny slut
Who was really a 45-year-old bald FBI agent
Judgment was in the air

It was two sixteen year olds
Who had held hands on the bus
Going to the basketball game
On the way home in the dark
Their moist lips touched
Their parents had found out
They were told to stay away from each other
I watched as they parted
It was obvious that they would meet again

As I gazed at all the naked women
In the magazine rack
I said a small prayer
That the obsessions and cruelties
Of life would die off
That the people using their power over others
Would lose it
That all repressions would be released
That desires bloom into sweet smelling flowers
I wished the young ones luck

I was taken from my prayer
The cashier was calling
Can I help you sir

I paid for my condoms and left

She Said You Never Talk To Me

They hadn't seen each other all day
They sat together
Started to talk
To share each other's day
He started to talk about something
He'd like to do
She said that she doubted he would do it
He recalled the times in the past when he had
She remarked they were fewer and far between
He thought about it
He stated he thought that wasn't true
He said he counted 5 times
That he had
She says She remembers 3 times
He gave examples of the 5
She said you like to exaggerate everything
With that
He said it was at least 7 times
She said let's call it 4 and drop it
It seemed on every sentence
She was doubtful
Correcting
He was trying to talk about his feelings
The numbers were meaningless
He fell silent
She said
You never talk to me

Hanging By A Deposit Slip

He was living paycheck to paycheck
The money came in
The money went out
He was just 3 days before the next paycheck
He had a few dollars in his pocket
He thought he was gonna make it

He was then informed
They didn't need him anymore
There was no more work
And no money had been deposited
To pay for the work he had done

He had no money saved

He looked in the mirror
Asked himself what's the plan
His ship was taking on water
He could feel it tickling his ankles
There was no more money

When his friends found him
He was hanging by a deposit slip

A Perfect Match

Everything is Beautiful married
Gloom and Doom
Many of their friends said it wouldn't last

Doom hates bright colors
Beautiful dressed like a rainbow

Beautiful wakes up with a smile every day
Doom needs to be dragged from the darkness

Each day the struggle is played out
Will the light shine in?
Or
Will the darkness take over?

Each day Doom struggles
Doom feels in their bones
Something will go wrong
Things will turn out badly

Everything is Beautiful
Has everything fall into place
Turns out better than imagined

Gloom and Doom & Everything is Beautiful
Went on a vacation
Out to the mountains on a dirt road
To walk some trails

Beautiful looks ahead with excitement
The joyous feeling of being outside
What a beautiful day for a hike

Doom is listening to the noises the car is making
Is sure the car will break down
Sees a cloud in the sky
There's sure to be a storm
Doom is certain they will get lost on the trail

Everything is Beautiful
Loves
Gloom and Doom
Doom says it can't last
It's been 20 years
Everything is Beautiful
Thinks it's a perfect match

Mercury Retrograding

Which one is it?
Mars,
Venus,
Mercury

Mercury is retrograding

Usually when Mercury retrogrades
All hell breaks loose
The shit hits the fan
Everything gets fucked up
Confusion reigns
Problems multiply like kittens
Communication breaks down

I thought it was just a regular day

Someone told me it's called Mercury Retrograding
Now that I know it has a name
I am wondering does it have a cure
Usually when things have names
Like diseases
They have cures
Some pills you can take
Shots they give you
Treatments that kill more than the disease
Maybe more pills
Then you're cured
Or maybe you'er not
You're a statistic
That's just the way it goes
Some call it
Mercury Retrograding

I Sent The Papers In Late

She wore a short skirt
She had long legs

When she sat down facing me
She turned her legs to one side
By doing this
She could spread her legs
And I wouldn't get a view

The problem was
She didn't sit still
She knew this about herself

Sure enough
She would be facing me
And spreading her legs

She'd become conscious of this
Her hands dropped down to her short skirt
She squeezed her legs together tight
And grabbed ahold of the skirt
As if to get it under control
To stop it from creeping up
She tries to pull it down
There was nothing to pull down
As she turns her legs away from me

I try to look at her eyes
Not watch her legs

With this short skirt
Her legs looked long

And they called out
Look at me
She crossed them and uncrossed them
And faces me and spreads them
Then her hands grabbed ahold of the skirt
She combines gripping the skirt and pulling on it
While tightly squeezing her legs together
As if to seal them shut

I started to ask myself
Is she trying to pull her skirt off?
It seemed pretty tight on her

It didn't seem possible
But her skirt did seem to be getting shorter
Then again I was trying not to look
But I found myself following her hands down
As she grips her skirt
To pull on it
In the hopes to make it longer
It never got any longer

I then noticed as she lifted up her hands
The skirt did creep up her leg
In this struggle with her skirt
I started to root for the skirt

Watching this woman
Pulling on her skirt
Has me wanting to
As she squeezes her legs together
I am thinking about opening them up

I found myself asking myself
Why was I here with this woman?

Watching her legs dancing
Spreading and squeezing
When I was taken aback
By her sudden question

What is your birthday?

She then handed me some papers
She said I needed to make 3 copies
To send each copy to the addresses listed
Make sure I put the correct fees
Owed to each agency
Otherwise it would hold things up
For another month
I took the papers
Suddenly realizing where I was
I turned to go
Then turned back
Asked a question
How much time do I have to get this in?
As she answered
I got to watch one more time
Her long legs swung around
Spread
Squeezed together tightly
Her hands gripped her short skirt
And she pulled

I sent the papers in late

I Am Not Looking

Out in the country
Where you hear crickets
Once in a while you'll hear a car
The wind going through the trees

There are reports of a storm
Thunder, lighting, hail, damaging winds

I am alone
No one is here to bother me
I can do, as I like
Just made myself a nice dinner
For a long time I didn't eat meat
Tonight I ate a steak

A Friday night
There was a party I was thinking of going to
I found myself wanting to be alone
I needed to get some food
I thought as I walked through the supermarket
Who is here on a Friday night?
It was pretty empty
Saw a few couples
Mostly singles
Many standing around
As if waiting for something to happen
A few not making eye contact
Others taking long looks

Standing in the same cash out line
A tough looking woman
Owning the space around her

Tattoos
Very short shorts, and skimpy little top
A face that wasn't bruised
Yet had seen many battles
I thought of Charles Bukowski
That this is a woman he would end up with
For the night
For the week
A few months
Years pass quickly
So many different types of women
I said to myself
I am not looking

It's One Think

It's one think
Did you mean
It's one thing
No
I meant
It's one think
It's one way
Of looking at everything

So let me get this straight
That's right
From one point
To another

What about the cinerary
You mean the scenery
No I mean the dead bodies
Laying along the road

Where's the punch line
It's on the way to the bank
The rich are laughing all the way to the bank

Talking To God – Costs Money

I was a young boy kneeling
Next to my mother in church
When she started to get up
I started to go with her
She turned and told me to stay kneeling
I asked her where she was going
She said to talk to God
I wanted to talk to God

I watched her
Walking up to the front of the church
She lit a candle
And knelt down
Soon she got up
And came back
I asked
What did God say?
She told me to be quiet
We went back to kneeling and praying

A few days later
I was driving by the church on my bike
I decided to stop
I found the doors open
I went in
I walked up to the candles
There were small ones and large ones
And I started lighting them all
I had a real bonfire going
I was really going to have a talk with God
Suddenly next to my side stood the priest
He asked

Do I have the money to light all these candles?
I put my hands in my pockets
And pulled out my empty pockets
The priest started to put out the candles
I learned that day
That it costs money to talk to God

Work Within Our System
The illegal Native

In a large building
In the heart of where all decisions are made
In one of the many rooms
Where the details are gone over
A group of men all dressed in suits
Sit at a table

Facing them was a man
Who looked very different
He didn't wear a suit
He was a Native

The Native faced the Suits and began to speak

The Native spoke in his native language
After a period of time he stopped

The Suits looked at each other
They had been sitting there quietly
The Native stood there silently
Waiting for a response
The Suits realized
That it was their job to respond
None of them were going to let on
That they didn't know what
The Native actually said
That they didn't even know
What the Native's native tongue was
This wasn't the first Native they had ever seen
They had no one to translate
There wasn't going to be a dialog

They knew the story
The first Suit began to respond
Let me see if I understood you

Is it your allegation
That the land is for everyone to live on
Is it your allegation
That you have no land
Is it your allegation
That it costs too much
Is it your allegation
That without land you can't grow your own food
Is it your allegation
That there is no land to hunt or fish on
Is it your allegation
That you have no place to live
You are on someone else's land
Which makes you illegal

The Native responds with more urgency
Then stops

Another Suit continues the questioning
Is it your allegation
That your people are being made into slaves
Is it your allegation
That there are no jobs
That the only jobs are for low pay
Cleaning up all our shit
That your people are poor
Not educated and in poor health
That there are no opportunities for your people

The Native spoke again with more urgency
When he stops

Another Suit asks
Is it your allegation
That the water that you need to drink
Is being taken
Is it your allegation
That we are making the water undrinkable
That your people have many diseases
Birth defects
Is it your allegation that
Water is being wasted
That you can't own water
That you have to buy water
With no money
Drinking water from the stream
Makes you illegal
Taking food out of dumpsters makes you illegal
Having no papers that say you can be here
You are illegal

The Native spoke with more emotion
With a defiance in his song
When he stops

Another Suit asked, are you saying
That the land you once lived on
Was taken for the resources buried below
That the land you once lived on
Was cleared of all resources it provided for living

That the land you once lived on
We needed to dump our wastes on it

That the land you once lived on
We have taken from you

Leaving you with areas unable to sustain life

The Native said nothing

Another Suit spoke
Now you stand before us
Telling us this is not right
Asking that we allow you to have land
To hunt, fish, gather food, and places to live

The Native spoke the sounds of eloquence

A Suit asked
Are you saying that
We owe your people an apology?
For what we have done
Plan on continuing doing
Am I correct in stating
That you are asking us to stop our way of life?

The Native stood silently

Another Suit responded
We want you to know we have heard you
We will bring this up at a future meeting
We will have experts look into these allegations
Our commissions will look over the findings
To see if the allegations are true
We will call you and tell you of the findings
These findings will be written up for all to read
Committees will be formed to create procedures
To address the matter
With that said
The Suit thanked the Native for coming
Bringing his concerns to their attention

He then wished the Native a good day
The Suit then addressed the other Suits
We need to move on
To other areas of important business

The Native then responded
Laughing
For a while
And then speaking in his native tongue again
It was quiet for a moment

Then one of the Suits responded
Am I understanding you correctly
That you don't believe
That we will do anything about this?

Then another Suit responded
Are you laughing at us?

Then another Suit responded
Are you threatening us?

The Native just looked

Before the Native could respond
Another Suit jumped in and said
You know using violence
Is not going to solve anything
Threatening us, getting all emotional and upset
Isn't going to create a solution
We need to not rush anything
You need to trust our process
So that the right thing can be done for everyone

The Native stood silently
The Suits said goodby
The Native stood silently

The men in the Suits were done
They had said what they were required to say
The Native stood silently looking at them

The Suits said they were sorry
They needed to move on
To other important issues before them
The Suits had given the Native his chance
To talk
It was time for him to leave
When the Native made no motion to leave
The Suits once again said goodby
The Native gave no indication
That he was going to leave
The men in the Suits
Called in the men in the Uniforms
The Suits ordered the men in the Uniforms
To take the Native away
For now the Native was illegal for not leaving
After the Native was dragged from the room
The Suits looked at each other
Then one of them said
Why won't these people
Work within our system?

Stacy

Today I found out that Stacy
The transsexual who used to work in the Post Office
In Greenfield, MA
Hung Him / Herself
I didn't know Stacy
I saw him in the Post Office
Where He first worked in the back room
He/ She would open up the door to get your packages
I had heard that she
Took the Post Office to court
Because She
Wanted to work out in the Lobby
She won
I remember his painted nails
And
Big hands
She was always styling in hot clothes
Never saw her with anyone
She hung herself
Her dog was found dead in the same room
So far no one has claimed the body
Just another day
In the land of the free and the home of the brave

He Hated Public Scenes

In an airport restaurant
A man and a woman
The waiter addresses the man as Boss
Hi Boss
How's it going?
What can I get for ya?

The woman says
Women are treated as second class
The waiter didn't call her boss
He took it just as a greeting
She said women are ignored

As they were walking
Through this unfamiliar airport
On the way to their gate
They were reading the signs
They came to one
That had their gate number on it
He read the sign and said the gate is to the right
She looked at the sign and said
No it's straight ahead
He looked again, read the sign
He saw the arrow and said no
It's to the right
And started to go
She called out and said no wait
He said to himself
Why did she always question?
He expressed himself
With a sound and body language

She asked him to come back
She said look at the sign
He looked again
This time noticed
The sign was broken up into two signs
One half had the gate info on it
Had an arrow he hadn't seen
It was pointing straight
The second half of the sign had other info
An arrow pointing right
He had read it as all one sign
So he said ok and proceeded straight
She was not done

As they walked through the airport
She asked why does he treat her this way?
He thought of it as just a misunderstanding
He read the sign wrong
She had been right
As they walked and talked
He realized he had deeper feelings
That she was always questioning him
She had deeper feelings
As a woman
She was always being treated
As a second-class citizen
This reading of the sign became the signpost
He wanted to just get through the airport security
She wanted to process
To him it felt too public
She said men hate
Having emotional public scenes
She was crying
She didn't have a problem crying in public

This to her was another way men controlled
Emotions were voided from public life

They processed
They made their plane
He hated public scenes

He Touched Her Shoulders

She fell in love
When he touched her shoulders

Everyone else
Had just gone for her breasts
They would
Squeeze
And
Pinch
And
Play with the nipples
Endlessly
No matter how much
She informed them
There were other parts of her body
And soul
Screaming out for some attention

They would go for the breasts

He went for her shoulders

For the backs of her arms

She was delirious with how many
Spots
There were

Six years later
378 Quarts of Scotch later
79 couples therapy sessions later
Unknown number of screaming sessions later

She realized
She fell in love
With how he touched her shoulders
That was it
They both tried to make more of it
She just loved how he touched her shoulders

We Each Longed For That Earlier Time

In the beginning
You were so cute
So sexy and handsome
And felt so deliciously good
While we embrace in laughter
With happiness and total bliss
At our finger tips

Time passes
And what was beautiful
Turnes ugly
And vicious
Feeling the unbearable pain
Assessing the damages to our heart and soul
Becomes our daily diet
We each longed for that earlier time

She Walked Into The House

She walked into the house
Her smile lit up the room
She walked right to me
And held herself close
My hand squeezed the cheek of her ass
And gripped her thigh
She kissed me
Like we had all the time in the world
We were soon climbing on top of the table
Why waste time
Our bodies pressed themselves
Against each other

She walked into the house
Said this was the worst day of her life
As she looked at me
Things only got worse
I said
Oh honey, Oh Sweetie Pie, Oh my Delicious
She said save it
I said Peaches, Scrumptious, Honey Dew
She said you didn't clean the dishes
I was going to
You said you were going to take off your boots
I am standing there in my boots making puddles
She said you were going to get a job
I say I am working on a plan
There are times when
She doesn't have to say anything
I can see it in her eyes
I look away

She walked into the house
I ran to meet her
Grabbed her in my arms
Told her how much I missed her
Sank my lips into hers
She pushed me away
Is that all you think about
I told her I had some other ideas
She wasn't interested
I ran out of ideas
She didn't notice
I hesitate running to meet her

She walked into the house
I heard the door
She said hello
I said hello
She said I am home
I said I am glad
That was it
We both had a long day

She walked into the house
Her eyes didn't even meet mine
My voice drove her into a rage
She kept her distance
Don't even think about touching me
Maybe sleep in separate rooms
Maybe pack my bags
Move to another state

She walked into the house
Her smile lit up the room
She walked right to me

And held herself close
My hand squeezed the cheek of her ass
And gripped her thigh
She kissed me
Like we had all the time in the world
We were soon climbing on top of the table
Why waste time
Our bodies pressed themselves
Against each other

One never knows what might happen
When she walks into the house

The Truth

She said
You don't expect me to believe
Anything you just said
Do you??

He said
On a good day
I would hope for 75%
It looks like it's not a good day
How about 25%

She said
Why not just tell the truth?

He said
Both of us
Don't want to hear it

It's Not Funny

Times are tough
Times have always been tough
A good laugh is always needed

Knock Knock
Who's there?
The FBI

It's not funny

A skunk walks into a bar
The bartender says
We don't want the bar to smell
The skunk says
Then clean it
It's not funny

There were three Holy men
A Priest
A Rabbi
And a Monk

A young child walked up to them
The three Holy men said in unison
Where do we find God?

The child said we are all God

The three Holy men laughed
They thought it was a joke

It's Not Funny

I Don't Remember

It was a large building
Where people
With Alzheimer's and dementia
Lived
From one minute to the next
Nothing was remembered

Yet stories about their past
Were told in great detail

Everyone got lost
Walking around the halls
Not finding their way back
To their own rooms

If the rooms at the end of each hall
Had their door open

They would fill up with people
Who all thought this was their room

They didn't remember
How they got there

There was a woman who came down every day
Sat quietly on the couches in the lobby
Would wait for one of the staff to talk to her
She would always say
There was someone in her room
That they were in her bed
Most tried to humor her
Get her tea

Change the subject
Every day she would be there
One day walking in the halls
One of the staff ran into this woman
She said someone is in my room and in my bed
They thought this is the perfect time
To go to her room
And show her no one was there
When they arrived
There was a guy in her room
He was in her bed
Just lying there
He thought he was in his room
He wanted to know
Why does this woman keep bothering him?

Everyone was led back to their rooms
The women who complained
About the man in her room
Was checked in on

Back in the staff room
Discussions about the craziness of the day
Someone asks
Do you remember the last time
We had a day like today

I don't remember

No You Can't

I have a little audience participation piece
And it's in two parts

The first part is simple
After I say
We have to say
You say
No You Can't

So let's try that
We have to say
No You Can't

Here we go

When it comes
To someone stealing
50 Billion Dollars
Destroying retirement funds
We have to say
No You Can't

When CEO's
Walk off with 100's of millions in severance pay
And the rest of the workers
Walk away with nothing
We have to say
No You Can't

Starting a war on lies
Spending Billions and Billions of dollars
No money for sustaining future generations

We have to say
No You Can't

When President Bush
Lies one more time
Telling us of his great legacy
His missions accomplished
Two wars
Depression
A huge deficit
Homelessness and unemployment
Waste, greed, and torture
We have to say
No You Can't

When Dick Cheney
Stole the presidency
Created secret prisons
Waterboarding
And the list is too long
We have to say
No You Can't

When they try to convince us one more time
That nuclear power is clean
Don't worry about the waste
That lasts thousands of years
About the pollution from mining of uranium
That Nuclear Power is green
And they're not talking about the glow
And they want to build more plants
We have to say
No You Can't

When it is suggested

That we give more of our money
To the banks, stockbrokers and CEO's
Who stole and wasted our money in the first place
To keep doing what they have been doing
We have to say
No You Can't

When corporations drain us of all our resources
So we are left with no jobs
We produce none of our needs
Our only role is to consume
While we are unemployed
When they say
They are going to give more bonuses
And do what they want
We have to say
No You Can't

While the rich
Keep getting richer
Taking from the poor
We have to say
No you Can't

Now here's the second part
The first part was easy
All you had to do was yell
No You Can't
Now
You have to do something about it
Make sure business doesn't go on as usual
And if you ask
How can I do this?
Just remember
Yes we can.

Whispers

I was just walking out the door

When she came up to me
And started whispering in my ear

Ssmsmsmsmsmsmsm

I didn't catch what she was saying

It really didn't matter

Feeling her lips tickling my ear

Her Hot breath

I just wanted

Her to keep whispering

Ssmsmsmsmsmsmsmsmsmsm

I move towards her
Leading with my ear
As if to say
I didn't hear you

She whispered in my ear again

Smsmsmsmsmsmsm

I wondered how many times
I could keep asking her

Before she stopped whispering and just tells me
So I acted like I understood
I said really
Ssmsmmsmsmsmsmsms

I said how do you feel about that
Smsmsmssmmsmsm

Finally I said
What are you trying to tell me?

She said
Pick up some toilet paper
Then she said
Hurry back

The way she said hurry back
I decided to cut my list by a third
Actually after buying food
The first thing on the list
I went home

When I walked in
I realized
I forgot the toilet paper

When I told her
She didn't whisper

Stimulus Package

I got in the mail my stimulus check
It was really small
It wasn't very much at all

I couldn't do anything with it
It gave me no resources
To make more money
It would just disappear

I actually noticed some small print
That said if I didn't send the check in
By a certain date
I would be responsible for
Hundreds of thousands of dollars
There were phone numbers to call
They were always busy
It said I could respond online
The website went in circles
Ate up hours upon hours
Waiting on hold while being told I was important
Finally I talked to someone
Who said I needed to be transferred
Which started the whole process over again
Luckily when I got through
This person said if I filled out forms f u c and k
And paid the filing fees
Which turned out to be under $20
I would be left alone for a while
So I filled out the forms and paid the $20

I had to admit
Looking back

Owing hundreds of thousands of dollars
Losing everything I own
Being homeless
But then was saved by a few forms

Was quite stimulating

Two Hands Under The Table

As we got into the booth
We both realized
We would be sitting next to each other

A night out with the gang
As we all squeezed in the booth
Both of our arms
Went to our sides
And gently
Our hands found each other
And slowly
Embraced
With each of us
Holding on tight

Two hands under the table

Magic

She said what's that in your pocket
I was really embarrassed
So I didn't say anything
Looks like you have something in your pocket

She asked
Are you one of those people
Who stuffs their pockets?
She said
It's not good to put so many things in your pockets
It can drag down your pants
I nodded
She said can I see what's in your pocket
I said no
Why won't you let me see what's in your pocket
I said we hardly know each other

So lets get to know each other
So we started to talk
Had nothing in common

She then turned to me
She said oh look
Your pocket's empty
How did that happen?

I said it was magic

His Tone Changed

Here I am
I made it to being 55

Tonight I went to a meeting
And hit an all time low
It was partly the meeting
But more about who I am
What I am doing
What will I do for work?
Is there any work out there?

After all these years
I am still asking
What will I do when I grow up?
Something about the meeting
All the running around before
Things that were important
Having No energy for it

Something is missing

The uncertainty of the money
Don't want to feel anxious
The choices that are presented
Just couldn't put my finger on it
Many hours went by
I need to step back

I started to flash scenes of my life
Where I felt embarrassed about what I did
As if I was fooling myself
That people were really laughing behind my back

That I was a hack
I have always been a hack
With dreams

I have always had these feelings

I look in the mirror
Losing my hair
The other day
Someone who hadn't seen me in years
Kept remarking that I looked so good and cool
That my hair was white, and long
His was dyed and short
He kept saying that my clothes were cool
He was in a suit and tie
Said he had respect for me
Looking the way I want
Creating my own work

His tone changed
When I asked him for some spare change

Read The Signs?

Along the way there are signs
They aren't the painted kind
They're the actions taken by governments
The environment that is created
People's everyday lives
Are living signs
Some times they seem unrelated
Yet if one was to add up the sum of the parts

It started with a threat
People felt the threat externally
Then internally

Security checks seem logical
Terrorism and espionage are
The new social networks
Fear and the lack of trust the daily diet
Spying and infiltrating seen as a necessity

Targeting individuals
The majority stays silent

Restricting and embedding the press
We are told gives better coverage and security

Creating a secret prison system
That allows torture
Setting up a military tribunal
Creating a paramilitary force
And setting up Martial Law
To protect freedoms we used to have
Please Read the signs?

Billy

Her eyes were closed
Her lips
Held me tight
She opened her eyes
And said
You're not Billy

When she had walked into the party
She headed straight for me
I had been just standing there
Thinking no one cares

I felt my heart pump
With all of the attention

Two people
Knowing there was no future together

She said
You're not Billy
I said
Tonight
Call me Billy

Shivers

I am not sure
How you got your hands in my pants
I guess I allowed it to happen
I don't remember a struggle

I remember a phone call
You said you dialed the wrong number
I ran over to make sure
You
Were ok

I wanted to believe
That you were obsessed with me
Not being able to keep your hands off of me
As it turned out
You said the heat had been turned off
You needed to keep your hands warm

I amaze myself at what I will accept

With small crumbs
I convince myself of a torrid love affair
That brings shivers up my spine
When really
These shivers
Are your cold hands in my pants

I Wish You The Best Of Luck

They were sitting around a campfire
An old man
And
A young man
They had been talking

The old man
Was doing most of the talking
He was trying to pass on
What he had learned in his life

A way of giving him a new life
Through this young man

He wished he had done some things differently
Not taken so long to like himself

He now accepted
His awkwardness
His feelings that he was a jerk
His stupidity
His obliviousness to the obvious

Then there was his selfishness
And the foolish attempts to gain power

The old man's conversation rambled
As they sat outside
By the fire
Under the big sky

Then a young woman walked by

The old man watched the young man
The young man watched the old man
As they both watched the young woman
She knew they were watching
She walked by

The old man was silent
The young man said
So what do you have to say about women?
The young man was hoping
That the old man could tell him
Some secret

There was a long silence
The Old man said
There is so much to say

You must love yourself
You must be willing to compromise
You must be willing to accept

But most importantly
You must realize
There is no secret
I wish you the best of luck

Take A Breath

I walk out on to the porch
To take a breath

My cat is on the porch
She looks at me
Waiting for me to fill her bowl
She meows

Like what the Hell
Why can't you remember?
When are you going to feed me?
You know the routine
The food is in the shed
You go in and fill my bowl
So why don't you?

We both look at the empty bowl

I fill it
She keeps meowing
She says now that it's filled
I have to fight off the squirrels
The birds
The skunk
The cat down the street
Life isn't easy
She keeps meowing
She keeps discharging

I had come out to the porch
To look at the night stars
Let my head clear

Instead I am having this whole conversation
With my cat
Which is not having me relax
I had come out there to relax

Relax
The voice was saying
Let your mind go away
Relax
Listen to your heart
Take in a breath
Yes this was a very expensive workshop
It cost a thousand dollars
We were all in a room
It was strange
The room was very quiet
You walked into this room and it was quiet
You noticed it was quiet
You could hear people rustling around
You could hear their clothes
Everyone took a breath
Someone farted
It smelled

The voice continued
You need to inhale and exhale
The breath of life
The fart had killed the breath of life

When I could finally breathe
They were announcing
We have breath of life t-shirts in the lobby

Before we left
We were given the bonus information

We learned how to take our pulse
So that we would know
That we are still alive

My cat meows
I look down
She realizes I'm not listening
She walks over and starts eating

I look at the stars for a moment
Take a breath
Relax
And
Go back inside

The Headlines

In an alternative newspaper
With its readership representing
Communities that promote social justice

The headlines read
George Bush, Dick Cheney and Crew
Are escorted out of the White House
In handcuffs

Why didn't this happen??
Why didn't this happen??

A stolen election
George Bush lied lied lied lied lied lied...
One of those lies got us in an illegal war

The 9 /11 attacks
The twin towers and the pentagon

The most technically advanced country
In the world
With one of the largest armies
With the most military toys
Thousands of planes

And there was not
One
Military plane to investigate
Why four planes were going off course

It was stated that we were unprepared
When the record shows over and over again

That kind of attack
Was talked about
Planned for
Then it happened

And it was said
"We never saw it coming"
"We never saw it coming"

Why do we spend godzillons on
Killing off the human race?

Is it a conscious or unconscious
Master plan to reduce the population?
Can we control our population in a different way?
And then there is nature
With its own "plan"

Does it feel safer?
If our lives are orchestrated
Into a reality movie
Where the emotions can be activated
Released manipulatively
So everyone takes the feelings as their own
It makes it so much easier to control the masses

The population keeps growing
Overcrowding is causing shortages
Depletion of resources
Wars over resources
When everyone is hungry
Those who are the strongest
Will get to
Eat

Their neighbor
In most people's hearts
The movie would be one of sharing
Getting along, helping each other

We have drifted
We were talking about
The crimes George Bush and the gang
Committed against humanity

Bush's Clean air and water act
Made the air and water dirtier

George Bush took the most vacations
Of any president before him
About 20% of his total time in office
Headlines in the daily paper
The President catching a fish
His big accomplishment
It is stated later
He even lies about the size of the fish

George Bush and the gang
Staged a Hollywood moment
Flying Bush in
Landing on an aircraft carrier
Gave a speech
With a sign waving in the wind
Mission Accomplished
The truth
The war was just beginning

Dick Cheney
lied lied lied
He shot a friend

Told the police he couldn't see them right now
He lied lied lied
Waterboarding
Secret
Not so secret prisons

Cheney was asked should we invade Baghdad
After the 1st Iraq war was started
He said
"NO
Because if we go into Baghdad
We will go in alone
No other country wants to go into Iraq
None of the Arab nations would go in with us

It would be a US occupation of Iraq
So we take down Saddam 's government
What are you going to put in its place?
It's a very volatile part of the world
The country could split up
Pieces flying off
To this group and that group

Only 146 casualties
Everyone was impressed
The casualties in the first Iraq war

The 146 families asked why?

Casualties
How many dead Americans
How many dead men, women and children
Is Saddam Hussein worth?
Dick Cheney said None"

As of May 28, 2009
We are in our 6th year of war in Iraq
We have "Officially" 4,304 dead Americans
Hundreds of thousands
Are reported dead
On the other side
We have 320,000 Vets who have brain injuries
Concussions from battle are often not counted

How many military personnel
Have been wounded?

25 percent of veterans
From the "global war on terror"
Have filed disability compensation
That's more than 150,000
The present number of 4,304 dead
Doesn't include vet suicides
That occure daily

Where are the weapons of mass destruction?

I don't want to take down your property value
But I think they are in your back yard

Weren't we going after Osama bin Laden?

George Bush and crew have left the White House
Not in handcuffs
George Bush was recorded, for history, saying
He was going to be happy
To be out of the limelight
He was going to miss the chef at the White House
He joked that he was going to lose weight
Since his wife would be cooking again

His wife countered
She thought he would be grilling more

He also said he would miss flying around
In Air Force One
Since he could go anywhere

That's what he had to say
After starting a war
Spending Billions upon Billions
Devastating the economy
Removing controls to stop greed
Bankrupting the society
Total disregard for the environment
Pushing aside concerns about the well being
Of the Earth and all living beings
Instead increasing profits for a few
While others lose their homes
Retirement funds
Jobs
High unemployment
Many freedoms trampled
And others taken away

It is a major disconnect
From the world around us
To not take responsibility
For how our actions effect future generations
Education is a key
And George Bush's education policy
Called "No Child Left Behind"
Left many students behind
And killed developing life long learners
With testing

It said in the paper
That George Bush spoke somewhere
For the first time
Since leaving Washington
It said he was given a warm welcome

Why?

In an alternative newspaper
That promotes social justice
The headlines read
George Bush, Dick Cheney and Crew
Are escorted out of their homes
In handcuffs

I Am Strong

In 1986 I took a workshop with Living Stage Theatre founder, Robert Alexander. We did some improvisational theater where we were given a few details to a "story". We were using the arts to bring an awareness to our lives of what it means to be "handicapped". I was told I was a boy with a "bad" leg, that I was having my father visit, I didn't live with him. Another actor was told he was my father and that he didn't like having a handicapped kid. We then just started the scene, afterwards we were asked to write what happened.

I am strong for my father
I hide my leg
I am not smart
I am strong for my father
I love my father
He only loves me when I am strong
I want to be with my father
He has no money
He doesn't want to be with me in public
I try to be strong
I am only strong around my father
I am very weak
I feel helpless
I want to take care of little animals
My father doesn't like little animals
He wants me to be strong
I love my father
I am strong

The End

If Life is a stage
I need to find a new theater
Get a new director
Refuse to read the scripts being handed to me
Check the audience
To see if there is a pulse

Take a deep breath...

Ladies and Gentlemen

Welcome to the only show in town
Take a good look in the mirror
For you're looking at the star of the show

Try not to be disappointed
There is no script
And I am afraid that if you are awaiting directions
It's time to take out your compass
You may want to
Get on a bus
Hop a plane
Stick out your thumb
Go to a new town
Find just the right place
The right audience

Ladies and Gentlemen

The show must go on
With those of us that are still here
As we remember those who died
This is not the end

Final Notes:

The following pieces were published in other publications.

"No Love Letter Today" was published in Silkworm Volume 3. The Annual Review of The Florence Poets Society 2008.

"The Note" was published in - The Fall Equinox 2008 - a beautiful annual literary journal of Stories, Poems, Essays & Art by Booksmyth Press.

Thanks goes out to my brother for his support and editing.

Thanks to my men's group for their editing and support.

Thanks to many friends, acquaintances and fellow writers who gave their time and feedback, stories and encouragement.

I hope you have been inspiried to create, use your voice

www.ingramcontent.com/pod-product-compliance
Lightning Source LLC
Chambersburg PA
CBHW051839040426
42447CB00006B/605